# OPERATION STALEMATE

## 1944 BATTLE FOR PELELIU

## DANIEL WRINN

# CONTENTS

# GET YOUR FREE COPY OF WW2: SPIES, SNIPERS AND THE WORLD AT WAR

Never miss a new release by signing up for my free readers group. Learn of special offers and interesting details I find in my research. You'll also get WW2: Spies, Snipers and Tales of the World at War delivered to your inbox. (You can unsubscribe at any time.) Go to danielwrinn.com to sign up.

# SEIZING "THE POINT"

On September 15, 1944, five infantry battalions of the 1st Marine Division embarked in amphibian tractors. They clambered across 700 yards of coral reef to smash into the island of Peleliu.

Marines in the amphibian tractors (LVTs) were told the

operation would be tough but quick. A devastating amount of naval gunfire had been unleashed before their landing.

The 1st Division Marines still had grim images of their sister division, the 2nd's bloody attack across the reefs at Tarawa—two months earlier. But the 1st Division Marines peered over the gunwales of their landing craft and saw an incredible scene of blasted and churned earth along the shore.

Geysers of smoke and dust caused by exploding bombs and large-caliber naval shells gave the Marine's hope. Maybe the enemy would become quick casualties from the pre-landing bombardment. Or at least, they'd be too stunned to react and defend against the hundreds of Marines storming the beach.

Ahead of the Marines were waves of armored amphibian tractors mounted with 75mm howitzers. They were tasked to assault any surviving enemy strongpoints or weapons on the beach before the Marines landed. Ahead of these armored tractors, naval gunfire was lifted toward deeper, more dug-in targets. Navy fighter aircraft strafed north and south along the length of the beach defenses—parallel to the assault waves. Their mission was to keep the enemy defenders subdued and intimidated on the beach as the Marines closed in.

Naval gunfire was shifted to target the ridge northeast of the landing beaches and used to blind enemy observation and limit Japanese fire on the landing waves. This ridge would later be known as the Umurbrogol Pocket (or just the Pocket) and was one of two deadly unknowns to command planners.

The other unknown was the natural traits of the Pocket. Aerial images showed it as a gently rounded north-south hill that commanded the landing beaches 3,000 yards distant. From these early images, this elevated terrain was camouflaged in jungle scrub, almost entirely unaffected from the prepara-tory bombardment and artillery fire directed at it.

But instead of a gently rounded hill, the Pocket was a complex system of sharply uplifted coral knobs, ridges, valleys, and sinkholes. It rose 300 feet above the island and offered superb positions for tunnels and cave defenses. The enemy had made most of what this terrain provided during their extensive occupation and defensive preparations before the Allied assault.

Another problematic issue for the Marines was the plan developed by Colonel Nakagawa, the Japanese commander of the force on Peleliu and his superior, General Inoue on Koror Island. The Japanese defense tactics had changed considerably from their defeats on Guadalcanal and Cape Gloucester.

Instead of depending on spiritual superiority, Japanese defenders would use their *bushido* spirit and *banzai* tactics to throw Allied troops back into the sea. Japanese forces would delay and try to bleed attacking Marines as long as possible. The enemy planned to combine the devilish terrain with a resolute discipline. Japanese soldiers would only relinquish Peleliu at a horrible price in blood to the Marine invasion. This wicked surprise marked a new and vital change to Japanese defensive tactics compared to what they employed earlier in the war.

Nothing during the trip to the beach revealed any elements of the revised Japanese tactical plan. They bounced across a mile of coral fronting the landing beaches. Amphibian tractors passed several hundred mines intended to destroy any craft approaching or running over them. These mines were aerial bombs detonated by wire control from observation points on shore. But the preliminary bombardment had disrupted the wire controls and the mines did little to slow or destroy any assaulting tractors.

As the LVTs neared the beaches, they came under fire from mortars and artillery. This fire against moving targets generated more anxiety than damage, as only a few vehicles were lost. But this fire did show that the preliminary bombardment had not eliminated the enemy's fire capability. Even more disturbing was when the leading waves of LVTs nearing the beaches were hit by heavy artillery and anti-boat gunfire from concealed bunkers on the north and south flanking points.

Enemy defenses on White Beach 1 were especially deadly and effective. The 3/1 Marines under Colonel Steve Sabol were in a savage beach fight with no means of communication to understand the situation. Japanese guns knocked out several amphibian tractors carrying essential control personnel and equipment.

The mission of seizing "The Point" had been given to Captain George Hunt (a decorated veteran of the New Britain and Guadalcanal campaigns). Hunt developed his plans, which entailed specific assignments for each element of his company. These plans were rehearsed until every Marine knew his role and how it fit into the company's strategy.

H-hour on D-Day brought heavier than expected casualties. One platoon was pinned down all day in beach fighting. Survivors wheeled left as planned, onto the flanking point. While they advanced, they pressed their assault on several enemy defensive emplacements. Pillboxes and casements were carpeted with small arms fire, and smoke from demolitions and grenades.

The climax came when a rifle grenade hit the gun muzzle and ricocheted into a casement, setting off explosions and flames. Enemy defenders ran out of the rear of the block house with their clothes on fire and ammunition exploding in their belts. Marines waited in anticipation of the enemy's flight and cut them down with small arms fire as they burned alive.

Captain Hunt's Marines held the Point, but his company

was reduced to platoon strength with no other nearby units. Sketchy radio communications got through to bring in supporting fire and a desperately needed resupply. One LVT made it to the beach before dark with mortar shells, grenades, and water—evacuating casualties as it departed. This ammunition made all the difference in that night's brutal struggle against a determined enemy's attempt to recapture the Point.

---

The next afternoon, Colonel Raymond Davis of the 1/1 Marines moved his Company B to establish contact with Captain Hunt to help hold the desperately contested positions. Hunt's company regained the platoon survivors that were pinned down on the beach fight during the day.

The newly reinforced company recovered their artillery and naval gunfire communications, which proved critical during the second night. That evening the enemy counterattacked the Marines at the Point. The Japanese were narrowly defeated. By midmorning, survivors of the two Marine companies had secured the Point and looked out on 500 dead Japanese soldiers.

On the right of Colonel "Chesty" Puller's struggling 3rd Battalion, Colonel Russell Honsowetz, commanding the 2nd Battalion, took artillery, mortar, and machine-gun fire from still effective enemy beach defenders during their landing.

The 5th Marines' two assault battalions also took heavy enemy fire as they fought through the beach defenses toward the clearing's edge, looking out eastward over the airfield.

On the right flank, the 3/7 Marines crossed in front of an imposing defensive fortification flanking the beach. Luckily, it wasn't as close as the Point position and did not suffer heavy damage. But its enfilading fire, along with natural obstructions on the beach, caused Company K to veer off their planned landing and end up out of position and out of contact. After the confused and delayed battalion regrouped, they used a line of large anti-tank ditches to guide their eastward advance.

Any further delay would be a disaster to the division. Momentum was the key to success. The divisional plan on the right called for the 7th Marines to land two battalions in a column on Orange Beach 3. As the 3/7 advanced, it would be followed by the 1/7. These units would tie into the right flank and attack southeast on the beach.

After a bloody hour of fighting, all five battalions were ashore. The closer each battalion got to the Pocket, the more tenuous its hold was on the shallow beachhead. For another two hours, three more of the division's four remaining battalions joined the attack and pressed the momentum that General Rupertus had ordered.

Colonel Puller landed his forward command group close behind the 3/1 Marines. He was ready to fight, even if his location would deny him the best position for supporting fire. With reduced communications and inadequate numbers of LVTs to follow in waves, he struggled to improve his regiment's situation.

His left flank had two platoons desperately struggling to gain control of the Point. Puller landed the 1st Battalion behind the 3/1 to reinforce the fight for the left flank but was hindered by multiple losses in the LVTs. The 1st Battalion companies had to be landed singly and committed piecemeal into the action.

On the regiment's right flank, the 2/1 Marines recaptured the west edges of the scrub, looking out to the airfield.

In the beachhead's southern sector, the 1/7 Marines were delayed by the heavy LVT losses. This successful early opposition was felt throughout the rest of the day. Most of the 1/7 eventually landed on the correct beach, but many Marines were driven leftward from heavy enemy fire and landed in the 5th Marines' zone.

This caused the 1/7 to join in with the 3/7 and advance east to assault prepared enemy positions.

The battle raged with heavy opposition from both east and south. In the midafternoon, Marines ran into a blockhouse (supposedly destroyed by pre-landing naval gunfire) but had not been touched and put up a strong resistance.

The cost in Marine lives and lost momentum by having to assault these heavily defended blockhouses was harsh and unnecessary.

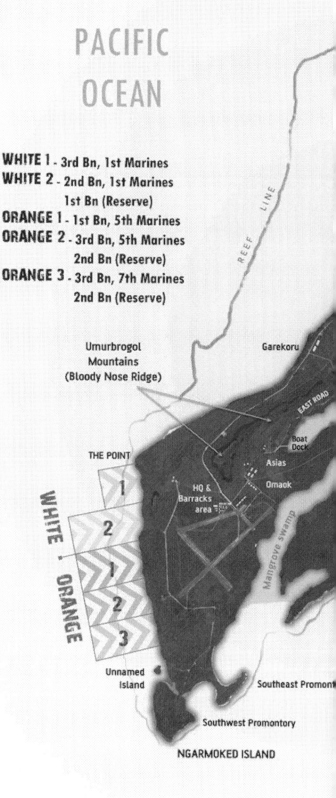

PACIFIC
OCEAN

WHITE 1 - 3rd Bn, 1st Marines
WHITE 2 - 2nd Bn, 1st Marines
1st Bn (Reserve)
ORANGE 1 - 1st Bn, 5th Marines
ORANGE 2 - 3rd Bn, 5th Marines
2nd Bn (Reserve)
ORANGE 3 - 3rd Bn, 7th Marines
2nd Bn (Reserve)

REEF LINE

Umurbrogol
Mountains
(Bloody Nose Ridge)

Garekoru

EAST ROAD

Boat
Dock

THE POINT

Asias

Omaok

HQ &
Barracks
area

WHITE , ORANGE

Mangrove swamp

1

2

1

2

3

Unnamed
Island

Southeast Promont

Southwest Promontory

NGARMOKED ISLAND

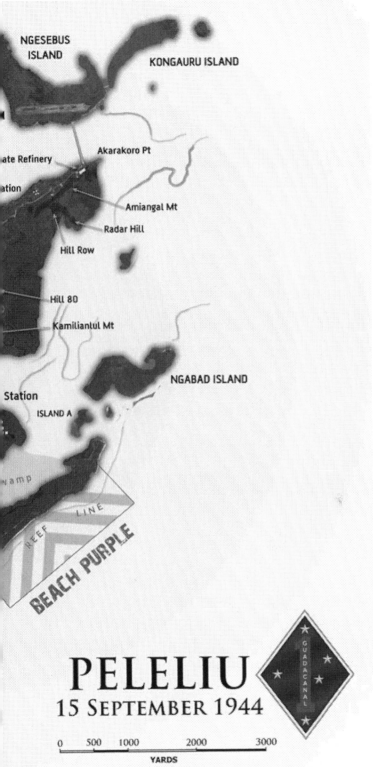

NGESEBUS
ISLAND

KONGAURU ISLAND

Akarakoro Pt

ate Refinery

ation

Amiangal Mt

Radar Hill

Hill Row

Hill 80

Kamilianlul Mt

NGABAD ISLAND

Station

ISLAND A

wamp

REEF LINE

BEACH PURPLE

# PELELIU
## 15 September 1944

GUADACANAL

| 0 | 500 | 1000 | 2000 | 3000 |

YARDS

MAP by AKHIL KADIDAL

# THE JAPANESE DEFENDERS

General Sadae Inoue, a fifth-generation warrior with a robust military reputation, commanded the *14th Infantry Division.* He'd just arrived from the *Kwangtung Army* in China. In March 1944, Inoue met Japanese Premier Tojo in Tokyo to discuss the war.

Tojo decided Japan could no longer hold the Palaus against the Allied naval dominance in the Western Pacific. Tojo gave General Inoue command of all Japanese forces in the Palaus. His orders: take the *14th Infantry* and kill Americans while denying its use to the Allies for as long as possible. He ordered Inoue to sell the Palaus at the highest possible cost in blood and time.

As the enemy sailed for the Palaus, Inoue flew ahead and surveyed his new locale for two days before deciding Peleliu was the key to his defense. The earlier Task Force 58 strikes confirmed his decision. Peleliu had been under the administrative command of a rear admiral. The admiral used his forces to build blockhouses and reinforced concrete structures above ground while improving the existing caves and tunnels under Peleliu's rich natural camouflage of jungle, scrub, and vines.

In these underground installations, the admiral and his troops survived the March attacks from Task Force 58. The above-ground structures and planes were demolished. when the Japanese emerged, they repaired what they could with a focus on the underground installations. Together with Korean labor troops, their numbers swelled to 7,000 (most lacking training and leadership for any infantry action).

Colonel Nakagawa arrived on Peleliu with his *2nd Infantry Regiment*—a 6,500-man reinforced regiment. They were veterans from the war in China and had two dozen 75mm artillery pieces, a dozen tanks, fifteen 81mm heavy mortars, over a hundred .50-caliber machine guns, and thirty dual-purpose anti-aircraft guns. There were many heavy 141mm mortars and naval anti-aircraft guns already on the island.

Colonel Nakagawa had been awarded nine medals for his leadership against the Chinese. His regiment was regarded as elite veterans within the Japanese Army.

Immediately upon arriving, Nakagawa reconnoitered his battle position from the ground and air. He identified the western beaches (the White and Orange Beaches) as the most likely landing sites. Nakagawa ordered his troops to dig in and construct beach defenses. But a conflict arose when the senior naval officer, Admiral Itou, resented taking orders from a junior army officer.

From Koror, General Inoue sent General Murai to Peleliu. Murai assumed command and maintained a liaison with

Nakagawa. Murai was a highly regarded, personal representative of General Inoue and considered senior to the admiral.

Murai left the mission firmly in Nakagawa's hands. Throughout the campaign, Nakagawa exercised operational control and was assisted and counseled but not commanded by General Murai.

Nakagawa fully understood his objective and the situation and firepower the Allies possessed. He turned his attention to making the fullest use of his primary advantage—the terrain. Nakagawa deployed and installed his forces to inflict all possible damage and casualties at the landing. Then his troops would defend in-depth to the last man. Peleliu offered a vertical and a horizontal dimension to its defense.

Nakagawa registered artillery and mortars over the width and depth of the reef on both eastern and western beaches. With a planned heavy concentration along the fringe of the western reef, he expected the Allies need to transfer follow-on waves from landing craft to the reef crossing amphibian vehicles. He registered weapons from the water's edge to subject landing troops to a hellish hail of fire. Offshore, he laid over 500 wire-controlled mines.

Nakagawa ordered the construction of beach obstacles using logs and rails and ordered multiple anti-tank ditches dug. He put troops in machine-gun and mortar pits along the inland from the beaches supported by all available barbed wire. He constructed concrete emplacements to shelter and conceal anti-tank and anti-boat artillery on the north and south beaches.

Inland, he used the already built blockhouses with adjacent reinforced buildings. He made them into mutually supporting defensive complexes and added communication lines in the trenches.

Nakagawa believed the western beaches were the most

probable route of attack. But he did not leave the southern and eastern beaches undefended. He committed one battalion on each beach to organize defenses. The eastern beaches were thoroughly prepared with contingents of defenders to move into central Peleliu if the battle expanded from the west as he expected.

Colonel Nakagawa assigned 600 infantry and artillery to defend Ngesebus and 1,100 Naval personnel to defend northern Peleliu. The only troops not under his command were the 1,500 defenders on Angaur.

The central part of his force and effort was committed to the 500 tunnels, caves, and firing embrasures in the coral ridges of central Peleliu. The naval units' prior extensive tunneling into limestone ridges rendered the occupants mainly immune to any Allied bombardments. Only an occasional lucky hit in the cave's mouth or a point-blank direct fire could damage the hidden defenses and the enemy troops.

Tunnels were designed for several purposes: command centers, hospitals, barracks, storage, ammunition dumps, and cooking areas with freshwater springs and basins—and of course, firing embrasures. He added elaborate concealment and protective devices including a few sliding steel doors.

Nakagawa expected an intense pre-landing bombardment. He believed his troops would endure it and carry out their mission of delaying and bleeding the Allies for as long as possible before Peleliu fell.

General Inoue was busy with his troops on Koror. He prepared for expected Allied attacks against Babelthuap. The Allied plan, Operation Stalemate, also called for the invasion of Babelthuap. As the expected invasion drew closer, Inoue made a statement to his troops, reflecting Tojo's instructions to bleed and delay the American forces. He pointed out the necessity to expect and endure the naval bombardment and how to use terrain to inflict casualties on the attacking force.

General Inoue said: "Dying and losing the territory to the enemy would contribute to opening a new phase of the war. We are ready to die honorably."

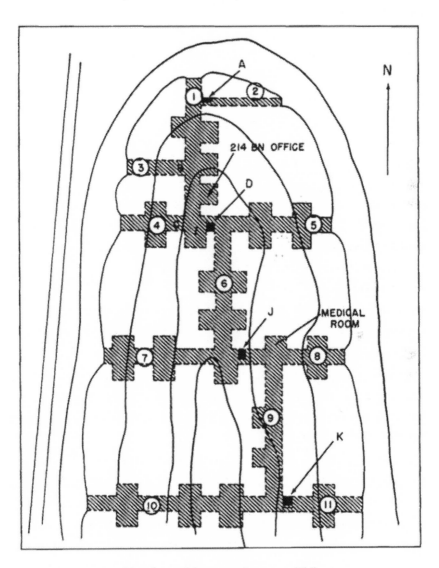

*Map of most elaborate tunnel system on Peleliu*

# D-DAY CENTER ASSAULT

The 1st Marines fought to secure the left flank. The 7th Marines battled to isolate and reduce enemy defenses on the southern end of Peleliu. The 5th Marines were tasked with driving across the airfield to cut the island in half, reorient north, and secure the island's eastern half.

The 2/5 Marines under Major Gordon Gayle landed on Orange Beach 2 and advanced east through scrub jungle and dunes. They moved in and out of the anti-tank barrier to the west edge of the clearing surrounding the airfield.

Gayle's battalion passed through the lines of the 3/5 Marines and attacked scattered resistance through the scrub in dugouts and bomb shelters near the southern end of the airfield. The 3rd Battalion's mission was to clear that scrub and maintain contact with the 3/7 Marines on the right flank, while the 2/5 Marines advanced across the open area to reach the far side of the island.

The 2/5 Marines advanced in the center and right, fighting entirely across the island by midafternoon. They kept contact with the 1/5 Marines and moved to reorient their attack northward.

---

The Japanese anti-tank ditch along the center and right of the Orange Beaches was notable because of the several command posts along its length.

The 1st Tank Battalion's M-48A1 Shermans—a third of which were left behind at the last moment—finally crossed the reef. These tanks had developed special reef-crossing maneuvers in anticipation of terrain obstacles.

Moving the fire and logistical support onto the beach was challenging and under direct observation from Japanese observers. This was an inescapable risk because of Peleliu's terrain. As long as the enemy had observation posts atop the Umurbrogol Point over the airfield and beach—there was no alternative but to advance rapidly and coordinate fire support.

The rapid beach advance caused heavy casualties. General Rupertus' concern for early momentum seemed to be correct. Marines on the left flank assaulted the foot of the Pocket's ridges and swiftly got to the crest. In the center, the 5th Marines advanced and secured all likely routes to outflank the Pocket. In the south, the 7th Marines destroyed the now cut-off forces before they could regroup and join the fight in central Peleliu.

The 5th Marines moved across the airfield to the western edge of the lagoon. They separated the airfield area from the eastern peninsula. They created a line of attacking Marines across the eastern and northern part of the island, believed to be the center of the enemy's strength.

Colonel Hanneken's 7th Marines pushed south and divided the Japanese forces. Hanneken's troops were fully engaged and mostly concealed against enemy observation.

It was becoming clear that the D-Day line objectives would not be met in either the north or south. General Rupertus was alarmed by the loss of his momentum, and he ordered the 2/7 (his last uncommitted infantry battalion), under Colonel Spencer Berger, into the fight. No commander onshore felt a need for the 2/7 Marines. Colonel Hanneken cleared an assembly area for them where they wouldn't be in the way.

General Rupertus was now fully committed. He told his staff that he'd "shot his bolt." On the crowded beachhead, more troops were not needed—they needed more room to maneuver them and more artillery.

Rupertus decided to land himself and the key elements of his command group onshore. His chief of staff, Colonel John Selden, convinced the general to stay on the flagship because it was too dangerous. So Rupertus ordered Colonel Selden ashore.

The shortage of LVTs stalled the timely landing of the following waves. Neither Selden's small command post group nor Berger's 2/7 Marines could get past the transfer line. The landing craft had to return to the ships, despite their orders to land.

At 1700, Colonel Nakagawa launched his counterattack. Marine commanders had been alerted to the Japanese capability to make an armored attack on D-Day and were well prepared. The enemy assault came from north of the airfield and headed south across the 1st Marines' line on the eastern edge of the airfield clearing.

This attack went directly into the 5th Marines' sector, where the 1/5 was dug in across the southern area of the airfield. Marines opened up on the enemy attackers' infantry and tanks. A bazooka gunner in front hit two tanks. The CO of the 1/5 Marines had his tanks in defilade behind the front lines. They fired on the enemy armor, running through the front lines as they advanced. The Marines' lines held, and they fired on the enemy infantry and tanks with all available weapons.

Major John Gustafson of the 2/5 was in the forward command post halfway across the airfield and had his tank platoon close at hand. While the enemy had not yet come into his zone, he launched a platoon of tanks into the fight. In minutes it was over. The enemy tanks were destroyed, and the Japanese infantry was ripped apart.

While Colonel Nakagawa's attack was bold, it was a failure. Even where the Japanese tanks broke through Allied lines, the Marines did not retreat. Instead, all anti-tank fire of every caliber concentrated on the enemy armor. Japanese light tanks were blown apart into pieces on the battlefield. Over one hundred were destroyed, although that figure may be exaggerated because of the amount of fire directed their way. Each Marine anti-tank gunner and grenadier thought they destroyed each tank they fired at and reported it that way.

With the Japanese counterattack repulsed and the enemy in shambles, Marines resumed their attack. They moved north along the eastern half of the airfield and advanced halfway up the length of the clearing before stopping to re-organize for the night. This was the farthest advance of the day over favorable terrain on the division's front. This advance provided the needed space for logistics and artillery deployment to support the next day's attack.

But this quick advance left a hole in the right flank. The 3/5 Marines were supposed to keep contact with the north-facing 2/5. But 3/5 command and control had been destroyed. The battalion's XO, Major Robert Ash, was killed earlier in the day from a direct hit into his LVT.

When the Japanese attack started, a mortar barrage hit the 3/5 command post in the anti-tank ditch and killed several staff officers and caused the evacuation of the battalion commander. At 1700, the 3/5 Marine companies weren't in contact with each other—nor their battalions.

The 5th Marines CO ordered his XO, Colonel Lewis Walt, to take command of the 3/5 and redeploy them in between the gap of the 5th and 7th Marines. Walt moved the 2nd Battalion's reserve company to his right flank in a tie-in position to form a more continuous regimental line. By 2200, he came under several sharp counterattacks from central and southern defenders throughout the night.

Enemy attacks came from the north and south. None had any significant success but were persistent enough to require an ammunition resupply. At dawn, dozens of Japanese bodies laid ripped to pieces north of the Marine lines.

Elsewhere across the front, there were more menacing night counterattacks. None drove the Marines back or penetrated Allied lines in significant strength.

In the south, the 7th Marines expected substantial night attacks from the enemy battalion opposing them. Marines were dug in and in strength. They had communications to call in fire support, including naval gunfire and star shell illumination—they easily turned back the sporadic enemy attacks.

At the end of the first twelve hours ashore, the 1st Marine Division held its beachhead across their projected front.

Marine positions were strong everywhere except on the extreme left flank. General Smith, from his forward command post had communication with all three regimental commanders. The report he received from Colonel Puller was not a realistic assessment of the 1st Marines' weak hold on the Point. This was because of Colonel Puller's own limited information.

Besides all three infantry regiments, the 1st Division had three battalions of light artillery emplaced onshore. All thirty tanks were also now onshore. The shore party was operating on the beach under sporatic enemy fire and full daylight observation. The division was preparing to press their advance on D +1. Their objective was to capture the commanding crests on the left, advance farther into the center, and destroy isolated enemy defenders in the south.

By the end of the day, at least two colonels on Peleliu had misleading information about their situations and gave inaccurate reports to their superiors. When General Smith finally got a telephone wire into the 1st Marines' command post, he was told the regiment had secured the beachhead and was on the objective line. He was not told about the gaps in his lines nor of the gravity of the 1st Division's struggle on the Point— where thirty-eight Marines battled to keep the position.

Colonel Nakagawa reported that the Marines' landings attempt had been routed. He also reported that his brave counterattack had thrown the Marines into the sea.

# THE UMURBROGOL POCKET

General Rupertus was irritated that after his failed efforts to land, his division reserve into the southern sector of the beachhead. Now he was informed that his northern sector—on the extreme left flank—needed reinforcements. Rupertus ordered the 2/7 into Colonel Puller's sector to assist.

Division headquarters afloat had reported the Marine D-Day casualties had exceeded 1,100, of which 210 Marines were killed in action. While not a substantial percentage of the total divisional strength, this number threatened the overall cutting-edge strength. Most of those 1,100 casualties were from each of the division's nine infantry battalions (with the exception of the center). General Rupertus was still not on the O-1 objective line—the first of his eight planned phase lines.

Rupertus had inaccurate information about the 1st Marines' situation. The general was determined to get ashore and see what he could do to reignite the lost momentum. He had a broken ankle from a pre-assault training exercise. His foot was in a cast, but his gimpy leg dragging in a sandy trench would not hold him back from seeing the situation on Peleliu for himself.

---

On Colonel Nakagawa's side, he saw a different situation from his high ground because of the incredible reports being sent out from his headquarters. The Marine landing force had *not* been routed. He watched while a division of Marines deployed across two miles of beach. While the Marines had been punished on D-Day, they were still in the fight.

Nakagawa predicted the next assault would be preceded by a hailstorm of naval artillery, gunfire, and aerial bombardments. Also, that they'd be supported by the US tanks that annihilated the Japanese armor on D-Day.

In Nakagawa's D-Day counterattack, he lost one of his five infantry battalions.

Across Peleliu, he lost hundreds of beach defenders in fighting across the front, and in futile night attacks. Still, he had several thousand courageous, well-armed and well-trained soldiers ready to fight and die for the empire. They were deployed through strong defensive complexes and fortifications, with abundant underground support facilities. Nakagawa's troops were determined to kill as many Marines as they could before they fell.

Colonel Nakagawa had the terrain advantage. He focused his defensive strategy around the occupation and organization of that terrain. Until he was driven from the commanding crests of the Point, he still had a dominant position. He could observe and direct hidden fire on the attackers while his forces were largely invisible to the Marines and their fire superiority. Continuing to hold this terrain was a key component of his overall defensive strategy.

The Marines were assaulting fortified positions, and precise fire preparations were needed. Marines on the left flank were under extreme pressure to advance rapidly, sacrificing speed for careful preparation. General Rupertus understood that enemy weapons and observation dominated the Marine position and troops were getting picked off at the enemy's leisure. Rupertus' concern for momentum was a priority and would save Marine lives.

The rapid advance burden was on the 1st Marines—on the left flank—and on the 5th in the airfield area. In the south, the 7th Marines already held the edge of the airfield's terrain. The scrub jungle screened the regiment from enemy observation.

Colonel "Chesty" Puller's 1st Marines had suffered the most casualties on D-Day. They fought through the most formidable terrain and assaulted the toughest positions. They had to attack and relieve Company K of the 3/1 on the Point and then assault the Pocket ridges north to south.

Puller's Marines (aided by the 2/1) swung leftward and secured the built-up area between the airfield in the ridges. When Puller was at the foot of the cliffs, his Marines fought in a savage, scratch and scramble attack against the enemy troops in the ridges.

Puller closed the gaps on his left flank and swung his entire regiment north. With the help of the 3/1, he reinforced Company K on the Point. Then he moved north, keeping his left on the beach and his right close to the West Road, along the foot of the Pocket. While the terrain allowed for tank support, maneuverability was tight, and hard fighting was involved.

The rapid rate of movement along the boundary and the more open zone created a pressing need for reserves. Tactically, it was necessary to press east into and over the rough terrain and destroy enemy defenses. That job was given to the 1st and 2nd Battalions of the 1st Marines and the 2nd Battalion of the 7th Marines. But more troops were still needed to move north and encircle the rugged landscape of the Umurbrogol Pocket area. By September 17, reserves were needed along the 1st Division's western (left) advance, but neither division nor III Amphibious Corps had reserves.

The 3/1 Marines battled up easier terrain on the left flank. In the center, the 1/1 Marines advanced between the coral ridge and an open flat zone. One of their early surprises, as they approached the foot of the ridge area, was another enemy blockhouse. Admiral Oldendorf had reported that blockhouse destroyed from pre-landing naval gunfire, but the Marines who first encountered it reported the enemy placement as "not even having a mark on it."

This blockhouse was part of an impressive defensive complex. It was connected and supported by a web of adjacent emplacements and pillboxes. It had four-foot-thick walls of reinforced concrete. The naval gunfire support team from the USS *Mississippi* was called on to help. They annihilated the entire complex. The 1/1 Marines advanced again until running into the far more challenging Japanese ridge defense systems. Major Davis, in command of the 1/1 Marines (later to earn a Medal of Honor in Korea) said the attack into and along the ridges: "was the most difficult assignment I'd ever been tasked with."

All three of the 1st Marines' Battalions battled beside each other onto the Pocket and its wicked, cave-filled coral ridges. The initial reserve, the 2/7 Marines, was assigned to the 1st Marines and immediately thrown into the fight. Colonel Puller fed companies into the battle piecemeal. Shortly afterward, the 2/7 took the central zone of action between the 1st and 2nd Marine Battalions.

The 1st Marines continued to assault the stubborn enemy defenders in their underground caves and fortifications. Every new advance opened the Marines to new fire from the incredible number of cliffs and ridges and concealed positions in the caves above and below the newly won ground.

Nothing exemplified this tactical dilemma better than the September 19 seizure and withdrawal from Hill 100. This ridge bordered the Horseshoe Valley on the eastern limit of the Pocket. The 2/1 Marines landed with 240 Marines. Now they had only 90 Marines left when they were ordered to take Hill 100. The Japanese called it East Mountain (Higashiyama).

Marines were at first supported by tanks but lost that support when the leading two tanks slipped off the approach causeway. The Marines continued with only mortar support into the face of heavy machine gun and mortar fire. When the Marines reached the summit at twilight, they discovered the ridge's northeast extension continued to even higher ground, where Japanese troops poured fire on the hill.

Just as threatening was fire from enemy caves on the parallel ridge to the west—known as Five Brothers. Into the setting darkness, Marines supported by heavy mortars hung on. Throughout the night, a series of enemy counterattacks on the ridge top were turned back. Marines repulsed them with mortars and hand-to-hand brawls, knives, and rifles. Marines even threw rocks when their grenade supplies ran low.

Marines were still clinging to the ridge-top when dawn broke. Only eight Marines were left. The remaining Marines, under the command of Captain Everett Pope, withdrew and successfully evacuated their wounded. The dead were left behind on the ridge until October 3, when the ridge was finally captured for good. Another example of the enemy's expert use of mutually supporting positions on the Umurbrogol Pocket.

By D +4, the 1st Marines was a regiment in name only. They'd taken over 1,500 casualties. General Rupertus had continued to urge Puller's under-strength Marines forward. General Geiger (commander of III Amphibious Corps and Rupertus' superior) was an experienced ground operations commander from Guam to Bougainville. He understood the lower combat efficiency that these types of losses imposed on a committed combat unit.

On October 2, General Geiger, after visiting Puller in his forward command post and observing the exhausted condition of his Marines, met with General Rupertus and his staff. Rupertus wasn't willing to admit that his division needed to be reinforced, but Geiger overruled him. He ordered the Army's 321st Regiment Combat Team and 81st Infantry Division (on Angaur) to be attached to the 1st Marine Division.

Geiger ordered Rupertus to stand down and send the 1st

Marines to the division's rear area base on Pavuvu, in the Russell Islands.

On September 21, the 1st Marines had 1,749 casualties. They reported killing over 4,000 Japanese soldiers and capturing ten heavily defended coral ridges. They reported the destruction of three blockhouses, twenty-five pillboxes, fourteen anti-tank guns, and over 140 defended caves.

The 1st Marines' assault battalions had captured much of the crest required to deny the enemy observation and effective fire on the airfield and logistical areas. Light aircraft flew on September 25 from the scarred and still under repair airfield.

With the Pocket now in Allied control, the division's logistical lifeline was assured. While the Japanese still had some observation capability on the airfield, they could only harass rather than threaten.

The Marine front lines were now close to the final Japanese defensive positions. While intelligence couldn't verify it—the terrain and situation suggested that all assault requirements had been met, and it was time for siege tactics.

Enemy defenders learned that when aerial observers were overhead, they could no longer run their weapons out of caves and fire on the beach or the airfield. After one or two rounds, they were answered with a quick counter-battery fire or a dreaded aerial attack from carrier-based planes.

On September 24, Marines used attack planes operating from the airfield on Peleliu.

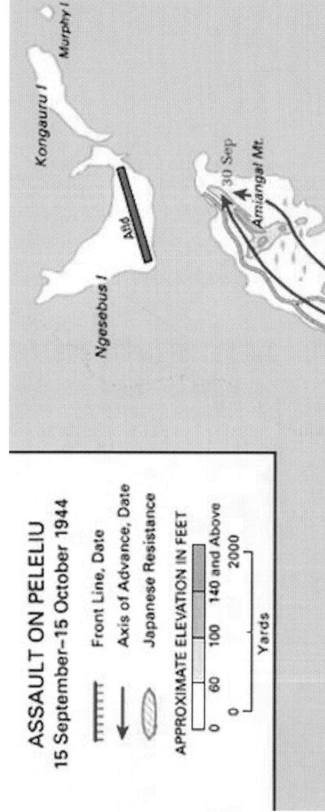

ASSAULT ON PELELIU
15 September–15 October 1944

Front Line, Date

Axis of Advance, Date

Japanese Resistance

APPROXIMATE ELEVATION IN FEET

0   60   100   140 and Above

0                    2000

Yards

Ngesebus I

Kongauru I

Murphy I

Atld

Amiangal Mt.

Kamilianlul Mt.

30 Sep

23 Sep

21 Sep

321st Inf
23 Sep

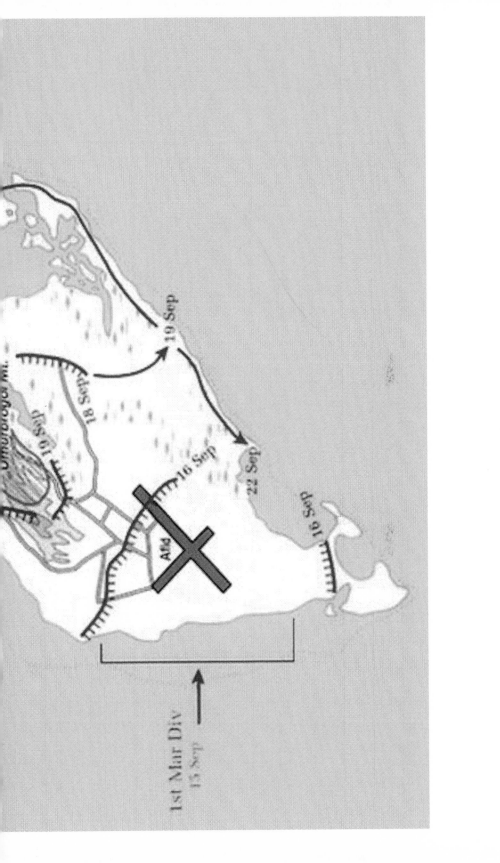

# PELELIU'S EASTERN PENINSULA

On D +1, when the 1st Marines launched their bloody assault on the Pocket, the 5th Marines (on the right flank) found less opposition and easier terrain to navigate.

The 1/5 fought southwest to northeast across the airfield through a built-up area similar to what the 2/1 Marines faced. The battalion took fire from the Pocket and assorted small arms from hidden defenders in the rubble-filled built-up area.

The 1/5's tank-infantry attack carried the day. Marines had control of the east to west cross-island road—the next step in securing Peleliu's eastern peninsula.

The 2/5 Marines had a more difficult time. Their progress was opposed by infantry from the woods, and artillery directly from the Pocket, which targeted their tanks supporting the attack along the wood's edge.

Whether the Japanese troops in those woods were posted to defend that position or just trying to survive was never established. The battle took all day, and Marine battalions suffered heavy casualties. By nightfall, the 2/5 Marines had fought past the north end of the airfield and halted to spend the night in the woods, concealing the approaches to the eastern peninsula.

The two-battalion Marine assault was deeply engaged on its front and right. Regimental headquarters near the beach was hit by an artillery barrage that, coupled with the 3/5 Marines' CO and XO losses, prompted a considerable rearrangement of command assignments. The barrage at the regimental command post took out most of the staff and buried the regimental commander in the crumbling Japanese anti-tank trench.

Luckily, it was a temporary burial, and the regimental commander, Colonel Harris, crawled out with a twisted and battered leg but could still hobble. Two of his staff officers were casualties, and the sergeant major was killed. Harris didn't evacuate but needed help in his CP. Harris ordered Colonel Walt back from the 3rd Battalion and had the XO of the 2/5, Major John Gustafson, take command of the 3/5.

Fortunately, the 3/5 Marines were having a quiet day,

unlike their hair-raising regrouping on the night of D-Day. After daylight, the 2/5 attacked to the north, and the 3/5 stretched along the east edge of a mangrove lagoon, separating Peleliu from the eastern peninsula. From that position, the 3rd Battalion 5th Marines tied into the 3/7 Marines as they attacked south.

This maneuver protected each regiment's flank against enemy movement across the lagoon and into the rear of the attacking Marines. While no such threat developed, a more pressing concern emerged for the 3/5 Marines. Major Gustafson was tasked with getting the 3/5 into position to bolster and relieve the 1/5 Marines as they closed in on their objective.

The next day, the 5th Marines tied in with the 1st on their left and secured the foot of the East Road. To the right, the 2/5 Marines hacked their way through the jungle north of the airfield and alongside a road leading to the eastern peninsula. A thick and almost impenetrable scrub reduced progress to a crawl. The scrub concealed most of the advancing Marines from enemy observation on the high ground to the northwest.

The 5th Marines' position overlapped with the northeast sector. Securing that visual boundary meant frontline Marines were spared hostile, directed fire from Pocket. Like the 7th Marines, hidden mainly in the jungle to the South, this would lessen the need for a frontal assault.

Now Marines had the freedom to maneuver purposefully and coordinate supporting fire more carefully into enemy positions.

# 7TH MARINES IN THE SOUTH

In the south, starting on D +1, the 7th Marines' spirited assault against enemy fortifications smashed into the elite *2nd Battalion, 15th Regiment.*

Even though the enemy was isolated and surrounded by Marines, this Japanese battalion showed skill and an understanding of Colonel Nakagawa's orders and mission: to sell Peleliu at the highest price possible.

The 7th Marines attacked. The 3/7 were on the left and the 1/7 on the right. Marines had the advantage of assaulting the extensive and well-prepared defenses from the rear—with heavy fire support. Both sides fought bitterly, but by 1530 on September 8, the battle was over. Marines destroyed the fortified elite Japanese infantry battalion in their stronghold.

General Rupertus was informed that the 7th Marines' objectives had been met, through the courage, bravery, skill, and many casualties of the 7th Marines infantry companies. Now the 7th advanced out of their successful battle area and into another bloody assault—better known as a siege.

The 5th Marines were still battling bitterly for the eastern "lobster claw" peninsula. By the end of D +2, the 5th Marines stood at the approach to the eastern peninsula off the East Road—near the 1st Marines' vicious fight at the Pocket.

They'd planned an assault on the eastern peninsula across a narrow causeway the Japanese were sure to defend. But a recent reconnaissance revealed that the causeway was not defended. The 2nd Battalion advanced swiftly to seize the opportunity. They moved across in strength but were turned back by friendly fire. The battalion was strafed by Navy planes, then hit by an artillery airburst that killed eighteen Marines.

Still, a bridgehead across the causeway was established and on D +3 the 5th Marines moved in. By the afternoon, Marines advanced to capture and clear the eastern peninsula. Marines expected an attack against a strong defending force that never materialized, this provided an opportunity to secure Purple Beach quickly—a massive logistical prize.

Just before dark, two companies of the 3/5 Marines moved across the causeway to plan the next day's advance. They hoped for little resistance but armed their point units with war dogs to guard against a nighttime ambush. Their lead companies moved out just after dawn, while nearly ambushed, the war dogs warned the Marines and thwarted the enemy's attempted surprise attack.

By the end of D +4, the two battalions had secured the main body of the eastern peninsula and reached Purple Beach from the rear. While the Japanese defenses were extraordinary, many were unmanned. The enemy troops encountered were more interested in hiding than fighting. This added to the speculation that Colonel Nakagawa's trained infantry had been moved west. By D +5, Purple Beach was secured along with the southwest and northeast of the long peninsula of Purple Beach.

From that position and others near the island of Ngar-dololok, Marines could direct fire against the cave-infested ridges of central and northern Peleliu.

---

Now that eastern and southern Peleliu was captured, the Allies planned to encircle the Japanese defenders in central Peleliu and assault nearby Ngesebus and Kongauru in the north. While this was the obvious next tactical phase for the fighting, securing it was unnecessary for strategic and tactical goals.

General Oliver Smith, the 1st Marine Division's assistant

commander, believed that the island's mop-up operations should take priority. He wrote: "by the end of the first week, the division controlled everything on the island that was needed, or later even used."

The airfield was secured and under improvement and repair—and in use. There was now no threat to MacArthur's long-heralded return to the Philippines. Purple Beach, Peleliu's best strategic axis, was secured and provided a protected logistic access to the major battle areas. While enemy defenders in their caves on northern Peleliu could still somewhat harass Allied rear installations, Marine counterattacks would quickly silence them.

Only two significant Japanese capabilities remained: they could reinforce Peleliu from Babelthuap and bitterly resist from their cave positions.

The Allied encirclement of the Pocket suffered from a lack of reinforcements.

The III Amphibious Corps reserves were fully committed to the seizure of Angaur. The Angaur operation's planning and timing were heavily affected by the Peleliu operation. Division planners proposed landing on Angaur before Peleliu, but General Julian Smith said that would cause the Japanese in northern Palau to reinforce Peleliu.

Division agreed that Angaur should only be assaulted after the landing on Peleliu was sure to succeed. But in the end, the assault on Angaur began before the Peleliu landing was resolved. The 81st Division's commanding general wanted to land as soon as possible and was supported by Admiral Bill Valenti. General Julian Smith argued that committing the III Corps' Reserve before the operations on Peleliu were more fully developed was premature and costly. Admiral Wilkinson ignored his advice.

On September 17, the III Corps' final reserve was assigned to the Western Attack Force and ordered to use "all available forces." Against General Smith's advice, Wilkinson committed the entire 323rd RCT and the 81st Division's other maneuver element. The 321st successfully occupied an undefended Ulithi, while reserves were desperately needed on Peleliu.

By September 20, the 81st Division had destroyed or cornered Angaur's 1,400 enemy troops, and Anguar was declared secure. The 322nd RCT would complete mop-up operations, and the 321st RCT was now available for further operations.

General Rupertus believed his Marines could do it without help from the Army. The III Corps' plan had the 81st Division reinforcing Marines on Peleliu and then relieving the 1st Marine Division for the mop-up. But General Rupertus refused to accept the help and continued to tell his commanders to "hurry up."

Rupertus also shrugged off suggestions from 5th Marines

"Bucky" Harris that he should take a look at the Pocket from the newly available light planes of the Marine Observation Squadron 3. Harris' newest aerial reconnaissance on September 19 changed his view of the Pocket from sober to serious. He believed attacking the Pocket from the north would be less costly than the original plan, and Rupertus told Harris that he had his own map.

The Marines' plan was built on the tactical concept that the 1st Marine Division would push in a northern line across the island's width after capturing the airfield. Once close to the southern edge of the Pocket, Marines would advance in four west-to-east phase lines. It was expected that the advance along with flatter zones east and west of the Pocket would be roughly the same pace as along the high central ground of Peleliu. Maybe this thinking was consistent with Rupertus' prediction of a three-day assault, but developments in Marine sectors to the west and east didn't change division-level thinking. Until additional forces were available, this linear advance may have seemed the only possible advance.

There was no re-examining the planned south-to-north advance, and for days, the Pocket was sealed off at its northernmost extremity. Still, the division commander kept ordering attacks from south to north following the initial landing plan. As "Bucky" Harris reported from his aerial reconnaissance of the overall Pocket, these attacks would only bring severe casualties. Heavily supported Marines could advance into "the Horseshoe" and "Death Valley," but their positions would soon prove untenable, and they'd need to withdraw by day's end.

The failure in this thinking may have come from the mapping use. The 5th Marines in early October created a newer sketch map to locate and identify the details within the Umurbrogol Pocket.

Even after General Geiger had ordered General Rupertus to stand down Puller's shattered 1st Marines on September 21, Rupertus made it known that *his Marines alone* would clear the entire island. After taking a closer look at the situation on the ground, General Geiger ordered the 321st RCT from Angaur and attached them to the 1st Marine Division—the encirclement of the Umurbrogol Pocket was possible.

Capturing Ngesebus and northern Peleliu became a priority. Allied forces discovered on September 23 that considerable enemy troop strength in the northern Palaus was being ferried by barge from Koror and Babelthuap. Even though the Navy patrol set up to protect against those reinforcements had discovered and destroyed some of the Japanese barges, many enemy troops had waded ashore on the early morning of September 23.

Colonel Nakagawa now had reinforcements on northern Peleliu.

# NORTHERN PELELIU SEIZURE

General Rupertus held a meeting with III Corps staff and General Geiger. They formed a plan to encircle the Pocket and deny reinforcements to the enemy on northern Peleliu. The Army's 321st Infantry would advance up the West Road with the 5th Marines. After they reached the Pocket, Marines would pass through Army lines and continue north to assault Ngesebus and northern Peleliu.

The 321st Army Regimental Combat Team was now a battle-tested and hardened outfit. They would advance up the West Road along the edge of the elevated coral plateau. The plateau was 300 yards west to east and formed the western shoulder of the Pocket. It rose seventy feet, and its western cliff was a jumble of small ridges that dominated the road. This cliff would have to be cleared and secured to allow for an un-harassed use of the road.

After the 321st passed this cliff, they could probe east in search of any routes to the eastern edge of Peleliu. Any openings in that direction would be a chance to encircle the Pocket on the north. Following the 321st, the 5th Marines would press their attack into northern Peleliu. The 7th Marines (relieving the 1st) were stood down on the eastern peninsula and relieved the 5th Marines of their passive security role. This allowed the 5th to focus on the capture of northern Peleliu and Ngesebus.

The West Road would be used as a tactical route north and then as a communication line for continuing operations. The road was paralleled by the jagged cliff, which made up the western shoulder of the plateau. This was *not* a level plateau and had a moonscape of sinkholes, coral knobs, and karst.

With no defined ridges or patterns, the sinkholes varied from room size to house size, and some were over twenty feet deep and covered by jungle and vines. This plateau was ninety feet above the road. And another 300 yards to the east, it dropped off into a sheer cliff (known as the China wall). Marines who looked up at it from the eastern approaches to the Pocket claimed the western edge of the plateau was "virtually impassable."

The plateau was also impenetrable to vehicles. Coral sinkholes forced all infantry to crawl, climb, and clamber into small compartments of jagged and rough terrain. Having to evacuate any casualties would involve rough handling of stretchers and the wounded men.

The enemy defended this area with scattered small units who bitterly resisted movement into their moonscape. Japanese troops ignored individuals and only fired on groups or what they considered rich targets.

The tactical decision along the West Road was to seize and hold the cliffs and coral spires. From here, they could command the road and defend these positions against any attacks. Once these heights were secured, troops and trucks could move along the West Road. But until secured, this cliff gave cover and concealment to the enemy. Until these cliff positions were taken and held, the Japanese could only be temporarily silenced from heavy firepower.

On September 23, this was the situation the 321st launched their assault into. Following an hour-long naval bombardment against the high ground of the West Road. Army patrols moved in and were screened from the Japanese still on the cliff. These small-unit tactics worked well until larger units of the 321st moved out alongside the West Road. From here, the enemy unleashed hell from above.

Two battalions of the 321st advanced along an east-west line across the road and up to the heights. Soldiers secured the west edge of the cliff and advanced northward, but some elements of the cliff were outpaced to the west. Instead of fighting to seize the ridge, some units responsible for securing the cliff abandoned it and side-stepped down to the road.

Colonel Hanneken ordered the 3/7 to capture the high ground that the 321st had abandoned. After that, the 3/7 Marines were committed along the ridge within the 321st zone of action. This stretched the Marines, who still needed to maintain contact to their right. Farther north, the 321st pressed on and regained some of the heights above their advance and held onto them.

On the northern end of the Pocket, the sinkhole terrain blended into regular ridgelines. The 321st assaulted Hill 100, along with a nearby hill east of East Road, and designated it Hill B. This position was the northern cap of the Pocket. The 321st would fight for Hill B and the northern cap of the Pocket for the next three days.

The 321st probed the eastern path across the north end of the Pocket. They sent patrols north up to the West Road. In an area of buildings designated "radio station," they found the junction of East and West Roads. Colonel Bob Dark, commanding the 321st, sent a mobile task force (Task Force

Neal), heavy with flamethrowers and armor, to circle southeast and join with the 321st at Hill 100. Below that battle, the 7th Marines continued to put pressure on the south and east fronts of the Pocket.

As this was underway, the 5th Marines were ordered to help in the battle for northern Peleliu. The 5th motored, marched, and waded to the West Road and sidestepped the 321st to join in the fight. The Marines found flat ground, some open, and some covered with palm trees. The familiar limestone ridges broke the ground. But the critical difference here was that most of the ridges stood alone.

Marines were not exposed to flanking fire from parallel ridges like they were in the Pocket. The Japanese fortified the northern ridges with extensive tunnels and concealed gun positions. But these positions could be attacked individually with flamethrowers, demolitions, and tank tactics. Many of the enemy defenders were from Naval construction units and not trained infantrymen.

On the US side of the fighting, Colonel "Bucky" Harris was determined to direct all available firepower before sending his infantry into the fight. His newer aerial reconnaissance gave him a better understanding of the terrain.

On September 25, the 1/5 Marines secured the radio station complex. When the 3/5 arrived, they were ordered to seize the next high ground to the east of the 1/5's position. From there, they would extend the regimental line back to the beach. This broke contact with the 321st's operations in the south but fulfilled Colonel Harris's plan to advance north as rapidly as possible without overextending their lines.

By suddenly establishing this regimental beachhead, the 5th Marines had surprised the enemy with powerful forces in position to engage them fully in their cave defenses the next day.

# 5TH MARINES NORTHERN ATTACK

On September 26, the 321st launched a three-pronged attack
against Hill B. The 5th Marines attacked the four hills running

east to west across Peleliu (Hills 1,2,3, and Radar Hill). This
row of hills was perpendicular to the south of the last
northern ridge—Amiangal.

These hills were defended by 1,500 enemy infantry,
artillery, naval engineers, and the shot-up reinforcing infantry
battalion, which landed on the night of September 23. The
enemy were well protected in the caves and interconnected
tunnels within the hills and ridges.

As the fighting started, Colonel Harris side-stepped his 2nd
Battalion west of the hills and attacked Amiangal Ridge to the
north. By dark, the 2nd Battalion had secured the southern
end of the ridge but took heavy fire from positions in the
central and northwestern slopes.

The Marines now confronted the most wide-ranging set of
tunnels and caves on Peleliu. They were trying to invade the
homes and defensive positions of a long-established naval
construction unit. Most of whose members were better miners
than infantrymen. As night settled, the 2nd Battalion cut itself
loose from its southern units and formed a small battalion
beachhead for the night.

The next morning, the 2/5 Marines tried to advance along

the route leading to the northern nose of Amiangal Ridge. They ran into a wide and deep anti-tank ditch that denied them the close tank support they'd successfully used earlier. Again, the 5th Marines asked for point-blank artillery.

This time division responded. Major George Hanna's 155mm Gun Battalion moved one of its pieces into position. This gun was 175 yards from the face of the ridge. The sight of that gun prompted enemy machine-gun and small arms fire, inflicting casualties upon the artilleryman.

Enemy fire was quickly suppressed by Marine rifle fire and then by the 155mm gun. Throughout the morning, the heavy 155mm fire pounded across the face of the ridge and destroyed or closed all identified caves on the west face—except one. That cave was a tunnel mouth that led down to the ground level in the northwest base of the hill. It was too close to Marine lines to permit the 155mm to fire on it.

After a bulldozer filled in a portion of the anti-tank ditch, tank-infantry teams moved into blast and bulldoze the tunnel mouth closed. Marines swept over the slopes above the tunnel and secured the crest of the northern nose of Amiangal. While Marines held the outside of the hill, stubborn Japanese defenders still occupied the interior.

A maze of interconnected tunnels extended throughout the length of the small Amiangal mountain. Enemy defenders would blast open the previously closed cave or tunnel mouth and surge out in a banzai attack. Apart from the surprise, these counterattacks were a rare and welcome opportunity for Marines to see and kill their enemy in daylight. These tactics were inconsistent with the overall enemy strategy on Peleliu and shortened the fight for the island's northern end.

As the fighting raged on, the 5th Marines assembled its 3rd Battalion with supporting tanks, amphibian tractors, naval gunfire, and air support to assault and secure Ngesebus 700 yards to the north of Peleliu on September 28.

This operation involved a single, reinforced battalion against 500 prepared and entrenched enemy infantry. In just over forty hours, the 3/5 Marines fought the most cost-effective single battalion battle in the Peleliu campaign.

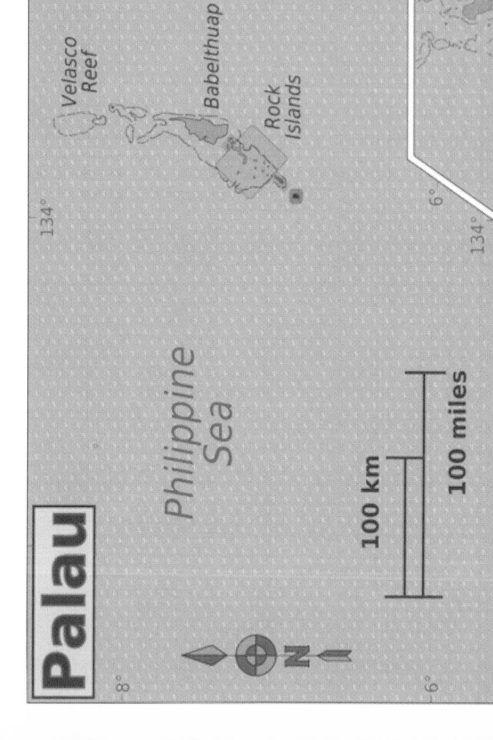

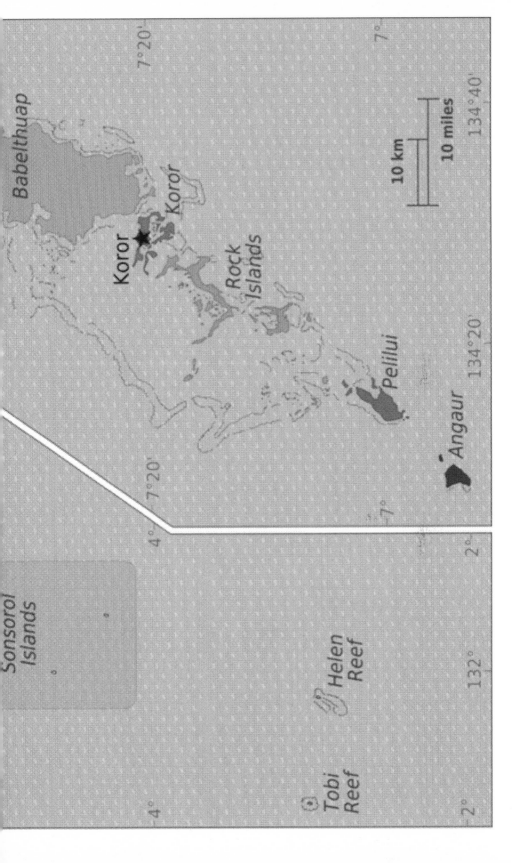

# SEIZURE OF NGESEBUS

The 3rd Battalion got ashore with no casualties. They immediately knocked out all the enemy's beach defenses. Then they turned their attention to the cave positions in the ridges and blockhouses. The ridges here were like those in northern Peleliu in that they stood individually and not part of a complex ridge system.

This denied enemy troops the opportunity to have a mutual defense between cave positions. The attacking Marines could use supporting tanks and concentrate all their fire on each defensive system—without taking fire from their flanks.

By dusk on September 28, the 3/5 Marines had overrun most of the enemy opposition. The next day at 1500, Ngesebus was declared secure. The island was turned over to the 321st, and the 3/5 Marines were put into the division reserve.

The seizure of Ngesebus by one depleted infantry battalion illustrates an enduring principle of war: effective concentration of means. General Rupertus concentrated all his available firepower: divisional and corps artillery, two cruisers, a battleship, nearly all the division's remaining armor, armored and troop-carrying amphibian tractors, and all Marine aviation on Peleliu.

This concentrated support allowed the heavily depleted 3/5 Marines to secure Ngesebus and destroy 477 of Colonel Nakagawa's battle-hardened, entrenched soldiers in forty-one hours at the cost of forty-eight Marine casualties.

As the 3/5 Marines were securing Ngesebus, the rest of the 5th Marines fought the Japanese still hunkered down in northeast Peleliu. After seizing Akarakoro Point past Amiangal Mountain, the 2/5 Marines turned south and swept through enemy defenses east of the mountain with flamethrowers and demolitions. Then they moved southward to Radar Hill, the stronghold of Hill Row.

Radar Hill was under attack from the south and west by the 1/5 Marines. After two days, two battalions were on the top side of the hills. But inside, there were still stubborn enemy defenders continuing to resist.

Marines solved this problem by blasting the cave and tunnel mouths closed—silencing the enemy forever.

# FIGHT FOR THE POCKET

The Umurbrogol Pocket was the scene of the bloodiest and most costly fighting along with the campaign's best and worst tactical decisions.

Its terrain was the most challenging on the island. Pre-landing planners didn't realize the Pocket for what it was: a complex cave fortress perfect for a suicidal defense. The southern slopes (known as Bloody Nose) dominated the landing beaches and airfield through where the Pocket had to be assaulted.

After Colonel Puller's 1st Marines conquered those heights through a costly and brave assault, command sent in artillery controlled by aerial observers. This radically changed the situation. The Pocket's defenders could only delay and harass Allied forces with sporadic fire attacks and nighttime raids. After D +4, enemy defenders in the Pocket could no longer seriously threaten the division's mission.

After more enemy observation sites were secured, General Rupertus continued to urge his Marines forward. He pressed his commanders to keep up momentum. As though the seizure of the Pocket was as crucial as securing the commanding heights guarding it from the south. But the challenging terrain and fanatical defenders became entangled with Rupertus' determined character.

This was only sorted out by time and the intervention of General Geiger. Most of the offensive into the Pocket between September 21-29 was directed into the cave mouths, ridges, and twin box canyons. Infantry, tanks, air support, and flame-throwing LVTs penetrated the low ground but were then surrounded on three sides. Enemy positions inside canyons and ridges were hidden from observation. Japanese troops were protected in their caves and were skilled at making the captured low ground untenable.

Other attacks to seize the heights of the eastern ridges were initially successful. Small infantry units scrambled up onto the bare ridge tops but came under fire from facing parallel ridges and caves. They were also harassed by strong enemy counterattacks who left their caves under cover of darkness in suicide attacks.

On September 20, the 7th Marines relieved the 1st Marines along the southwest front of the Pocket and resumed the attack the next day. These assaults achieved limited success behind heavy fire support and smoke. But these positions became impossible to maintain after the fire support and smoke lifted. Assault troops were withdrawn under renewed fire support to their original jump-off positions. There was little to show for the day's bloody fighting.

On September 22, against the west shoulder of the Pocket (Wildcat Bowl), Allied troops gained ground on their early advances—most of which were surrendered at day's end. Marines came under heavy fire from concealed defenders in their mutually supporting cave positions. The 7th Marines had advanced to within a hundred yards of Colonel Nakagawa's cave position. But several supporting hilltops and ridges would have to be reduced before a direct attack on the cave would have any hope of success.

The fight for the Pocket was turning into a siege, but the 1st Marine Division believed they could break through enemy opposition. Rupertus ordered continued battalion and regimental assaults believing they would soon bring victory.

When the 321st's eastward probes brought them within grasp of sealing off the Pocket from the north, they deployed two battalions to complete the encirclement. This assault would absorb the 321st Infantry's full attention until September 26, while the 5th Marines were fighting in northern Peleliu. The 7th Marines continued to pressure the Pocket from the south. When the 321st broke through on the 26th, their mission was expanded to assault the Pocket from the north.

The 321st broke through in the north and cleared the sporadically defended Kamilianlul Ridge. Their attack along adjacent ridges allowed for the Allied forces' consolidation on the north side of the Pocket—now 400 yards wide. On September 29, the 7th Marines were ordered to relieve the Army units in the northern sector.

Now that the 2/7 and 3/7 Marines were on static guard duty, hundreds of non-infantry were stripped from combat positions and put into support units. These "infantillery" units were assigned to hold the earlier held sectors. They faced the karst plateau between the Pocket and West Road.

On the 30th, with the 7th Marines' flexibility restored, they moved south and secured Boyd and Walt's Ridge. They controlled the East Road, but enemy defenders still harassed them from caves on the west side.

On October 3, the 7th Marines organized a four-battalion attack. This plan called for the 1/7 and 3/7 to attack Boyd's Ridge from the north, while the 2/7 would attack Walt's Ridge from the south. The 3/5 would make a diversionary southern attack into Horseshoe Canyon and Five Sisters to its west.

This regimental attack committed four battalions (closer to company strength) against the heights in the southern edge of the Pocket. The assault succeeded, but with heavy casualties. Four of the Five Sisters were scaled but were untenable and had to be abandoned. The next day, the 7th Marines made another attack to seize—then give up positions on Five Sisters.

During this fight, the 3/7 Marines' push led to a rapid advance that gained them Hill 120. They hoped this would provide a jump-off point for the next day's operation against the ridge to the west. But Hill 120, as with so many others in the Pocket, came under enemy crossfire, making it completely untenable.

The 3/7 withdrew and suffered heavy casualties. Among these was Captain "Jamo" Shanley, who commanded Company L. When several of his men fell wounded, Captain Shanley dashed forward under heavy fire to rescue two men, bringing them behind a tank. When he returned to help another wounded Marine, a mortar round exploded behind him—killing him instantly. His XO was shot by a Japanese sniper when he ran up to help, but collapsed on top of Shanley with a bullet in his brain.

Captain Shanley was awarded a gold star for the Navy Cross he earned in Operation Backhander at Cape Gloucester on New Britain, where he led his company in the seizure of Hill 660 in the Borgen Bay area.

The 7th Marines had been in the savage Umurbrogol Pocket struggle for two weeks. Under the *advice* of General Geiger, Rupertus relieved them but was still determined to have his Marines secure the Pocket and turned to his only remaining regiment. Colonel Harris moved in with his 5th Marines. He planned to attack from the north and chip off one ridge at a time.

# SUBDUING THE POCKET

On September 30, Peleliu aerial reconnaissance convinced Allied planners that siege tactics were required to clear positions in the Pocket. Colonel Harris believed in being lavish with ammunition and stingy with Marine lives. Harris would use all available fire support before ordering advances.

The 2/5 Marines were in position on October 5, but only reconnoitered positions where heavier firepower could come into play. Bulldozers prepared paths on the north end of the box canyons for tanks and LVT flamethrowers to operate. Light artillery batteries were placed along the West Road to fire point-blank into cliffs at the north end of the Pocket.

Cliffs considered "troublesome" were obliterated by direct fire. The rubble created a ramp for tanks to climb into better firing positions. Light mortars were used to strip vegetation from areas with suspected enemy caves. Planes loaded with napalm-filled belly tanks were also used to bomb enemy targets selected by the 5th Marines as their key objective.

While the 2/5 Marines picked off enemy firing positions in the north, on October 7, the 3/5 assaulted Horseshoe Ridge with tanks. This time the mission wasn't to seize and hold but to destroy all targets on the faces of Five Sisters and the lower western face of Hill 100.

When all the ammunition was used, tanks withdrew to rearm and then returned accompanied by flame-throwing LVTs and small infantry fire teams. This tactic killed many cave-dwelling Japanese, along with finally silencing their heavy weapons. Before this, single enemy artillery pieces firing from Horseshoe Ridge had harassed the airfield. After the October 7 assaults, no further enemy attacks occurred.

For six more days, the 5th Marines provided all available support to small incremental advances from the north. Light mortars were used to clear vegetation and routes of advance. Both tanks and artillery were used at point-blank range, firing into suspected caves or rough coral areas.

Napalm aerial bombardments cleared vegetation and drove the Japanese defenders farther back into their caves. All advances were limited and aimed at seizing new firing positions. Small platoons and squads made these advances. After Hill 140 was taken, they had a firing site for a 75mm howitzer. The howitzer was wrestled in, disassembled, reassembled, sandbagged, and then fired from position. The 75mm fired into the mouth of a huge cave at the base of the next ridge from where enemy fire had come from for days.

Sandbagging the 75mm howitzer posed several problems. The only available loose sand or dirt had to be carried in from the beach or came from occasional debris slides. The use of sandbags in forward infantry positions increased, and this technique was later widely used when the 81st Infantry Division took over Pocket operations.

# SECURING THE EASTERN RIDGES

The 2/5 carefully advanced through several small ridges and knobs and finally seized two murderous box canyons. Direct fire could now be poured into the west face of Boyd and Walt Ridges. But these cave-filled western slopes were protected by other caves on the parallel ridge known as Five Brothers.

After a week of siege-like activity pushed the northern boundary of the Pocket another 600 yards south, the 3/5 Marines were called in to relieve the 2/5. The forward positions being relieved were so close to the enemy that snipers picked off several incoming Marines (even the company commander).

During this exchange, a small enemy group reoccupied a position earlier secured by frequent interdiction fires. Even through these losses and interruptions, the relief was completed on schedule, and on October 13, the 3/5 Marines continued their slow and deliberate advance.

Terrain prohibited any advance south of Hill 140, so the 3/5 shifted southwest, paralleling the West road and into the coral badlands. This terrain was earlier judged unsuitable, but with the aid of fire-scouring napalm bombs, it was traversed. Major "Cowboy" Stout's VMF-114 bombs fell incredibly close to the advancing 3/5 Marines front and the stationary units east of the West Road.

The 1/7 Marines launched a similar effort. Together, these two battalions advanced and secured one-half of the depth of the coral badlands. Between the West Road and the China Wall this clearing allowed the "infantillery" unit to advance their lines eastward and then hold as far as the infantry had cleared.

In early October, the 5th and 7th Marines' actions had reduced the Pocket to an oval shape 700 yards north to south and 350 yards east to west. According to Colonel Nakagawa's radio report, he still had over 700 troops within the Pocket, and eighty percent were still effective.

Division command suggested enclosing the Pocket with

barbed wire and designating it as a prisoner of war closure. The Pocket no longer counted in the strategic balance nor in completing the effective seizure of Peleliu. General Rupertus wanted to subdue the Pocket before turning it over to General Mueller's 81st Army Division for mop-up operations. Rupertus' successful seizure of northern Peleliu and Ngesebus had ended the enemy's capability to reinforce the isolated Japanese troops on Peleliu.

Without pressing for a declaration that Peleliu had been secured (which would formalize the completion of the 1st Marine Division's mission), General Geiger ordered Rupertus to relieve the 5th and 7th Marines with his freshest and largest infantry regiment, the 321st RCT (still attached to the 1st Marine Division). General Rupertus replied that "very shortly," his Marines would subdue and secure the Pocket.

Admiral Nimitz sent a message to General Geiger. He directed him to turn command over to General Mueller's 81st Division, relieve the 1st Marine Division, and begin mop-up operations and garrison duty on Peleliu.

# MOPPING UP PELELIU

On October 20, General Mueller took responsibility for mop up operations on Peleliu. He described the tactical situation as a siege—and ordered his troops to proceed accordingly.

For six weeks, his two infantry regiments, the 322nd and 323rd, plus the 2nd Battalion of the 321st Regiment, did just that. They used sandbags as an assault device, carrying sand up from the beaches and inching them forward. They pressed closer to enemy caves and dug-in strong points. They used tanks and flamethrowers and even improved on the vehicle-mounted flamethrower. They made a gasoline pipeline from a road-bound gas truck, enabling them (with booster pumps) to launch napalm hundreds of feet into the enemy's defensive area. They took advantage of the 75mm howitzer on Hill 140 and found other sites to put howitzers and fire point-blank into enemy caves.

To support the growing need for sandbags on ridge-top foxholes, army engineers strung high lines to transport them (along with ammo and rations) up to the peaks and ridge tops. Army troops still took casualties, even with these siege tactics, as they ground down the stubborn Japanese defenses. The Umurbrogol Pocket siege consumed the 81st Division's full attention and both regimental combat teams until November 27, 1944.

This prolonged siege operation was carried out within twenty miles of a much larger enemy force of 25,000 soldiers in the northern Palaus. The US Navy had the enemy isolated with patrols and bombing from Marine Aircraft Group 11 operating from Peleliu.

As costly and challenging as the Allied advances were, Japanese defenders had similar demanding, and even more discouraging, situations in their underground positions. Sanitation was crude. They had little to no water, rations were nearly nonexistent, and ammunition was even more scarce. As time wore on, some Japanese were given the opportunity to leave the defenses and make suicidal banzai night attacks. Very few were ever captured.

In late November, General Murai suggested in a radio message to General Inoue on Koror to make one final banzai attack for the honor of the empire. Inoue turned him down. By this time, Nakagawa's only external communications were by radio to Koror. As he'd expected, all local wire communications were destroyed.

Tanks and infantry carefully pressed on in their relentless advance. The 81st Divisions' engineers improved the roads and ramps leading into the heart of the final Japanese position. Flamethrower and tank attacks steadily reduced each cave position as the infantry pushed its foxhole sandbags forward.

On November 24, Colonel Nakagawa sent his final message to Koror. He'd burned the colors of the *2nd Infantry Regiment* and split the remaining fifty-six men into seventeen infiltration parties. They would slip through Allied lines and "attack the enemy everywhere."

On the night of November 24, twenty-five Japanese soldiers (including two officers) were killed. One soldier was captured the following day. His interrogation, along with post-war records, revealed that General Murai and Colonel Naka-gawa committed *Seppuku* (Japanese ritual suicide by disembow-elment) in their command post.

The final two-day advance of the 81st Division was indeed now a mop-up operation. Carefully conducted to eliminate any holdout opposition. By noon on November 27, north-moving units, guarded by other infantry units, met face-to-face with the battalion moving south near the Japanese command post. Colonel Arthur Watson, commanding the 323rd, reported to General Mueller that the operation was over.

---

The tenacious determination of the enemy was symbolized by the last thirty-three prisoners captured on Peleliu. In March 1947, a small Marine guard attached to a navy garrison on the island found unmistakable signs of a Japanese military pres-ence in a cave.

Patrols captured a straggler, a Japanese sailor who said there were thirty-three Japanese soldiers under the command of Lieutenant Yamaguchi. While the straggler reported some dissension in the ranks, a final banzai attack was still under consideration.

The Navy garrison commander moved his personnel and their dependents to a secure area and radioed Guam for rein-forcements and a Japanese war crimes witness. Admiral Michio Sumikawa flew in and traveled by Jeep along the roads near the suspected enemy positions. Through a loudspeaker, he recited the existing situation.

No response. The Japanese sailor who'd been captured earlier went back to the cave armed with letters from Japanese families and former officers on the Palaus, informing the hold-outs that the war was indeed over.

On April 21, 1947, the holdouts surrendered. Lieutenant Yamaguchi led a haggard twenty-six soldiers to a position of eighty battle-dressed Marines. Yamaguchi bowed and handed over his sword to the on-scene US Navy commander.

# CONDITIONS ON PELELIU

Robert "Pepper" Martin from *Time* magazine was one of the few civilian correspondents who chose to share the fate of the

Marines on Peleliu. He wrote the following account: "Peleliu was a horrible place. Suffocating heat and sporadic rain—a muggy rain that brings no relief—only more misery. Coral rocks soak up heat during the day, and it's only slightly cooler at night.

"The Marines were in the finest possible physical condition, but they wilted on Peleliu. By the fourth day, there were as many casualties from heat as from wounds. Peleliu was worse than Guam in its bloodiness, climate, terror, and tenacity of the Japs. The sheer brutality and fatigue has surpassed anything yet seen in the Pacific, indeed from the standpoint of troops involved in the time taken to make the island secure.

"On the second day, the temperature had reached 105 degrees in the shade. There was little to no shade in most places where the fighting was going on, and arguably there was no breeze anywhere. It lingered at that level of heat as days dragged by (temperatures were recorded as high as 115 degrees).

"The water supply was a serious problem from the start. While this had been anticipated, the solution proved less complicated than expected. Engineers discovered productive wells could be drilled almost anywhere on low ground. Personnel semi-permanently stationed at the beach found that even shallow holes dug in the sand would yield a mildly repulsive liquid that could be purified for drinking with halazone tablets.

"It continued to be necessary to supply the assault troops from scoured out oil drums and 5-gallon fuel cans. But steaming out the oil drums didn't remove the oil, which resulted in many troops drinking water and getting sick. When the captains of the ships in the transport area learned of this and the shortage of water, they rushed cases of fruit and fruit drinks to the beaches to ease the problem.

"The water situation was a problem for troops operating on the relatively open and level ground. Once the fighting entered the ridges, just traversing the difficult terrain without having to fight caused the debility rate to shoot up quickly. An emergency call was sent to all the ships offshore—requisitioning every available salt tablet for the 1st Marines."

The statement that heat casualties equaled wound casualties was misleading. Most evacuated troops were returned to duty after a day or two of rest. Their absence from the front lines did not permanently impair the combat efficiency of their units. But these several cases strained the already overburdened medical core.

# III AMPHIBIOUS CORPS

The III Amphibious Corps commander, General Roy Geiger, was responsible for planning the seizure of the southern Palaus (Peleliu, Ngesebus, and Angaur). But Geiger and his staff were distracted during these critical planning weeks with the liberation of Guam on August 10.

The Guam operation took a month longer than planned. Someone else needed to plan the assault for the operation in the Palaus. A temporary headquarters, X-Ray Corps, under General Julian Smith was formed. The two main assaults of the southern Palaus campaign were assigned to the Army's 81st Infantry (Angaur) and the 1st Marine Division (Peleliu-Ngesebus). The 81st Division was also tasked with placing one regimental combat team as a core reserve.

While this separation of division level planning was convenient, it caused a gross imbalance of force allocation, neither recognized nor corrected as plans progressed. The 1st Marine Division had nine infantry battalions (8,000 Marines) to attack over 10,000 enemy defenders on Peleliu. General Mueller's 81st Infantry Division had six infantry battalions (5,400 soldiers) allocated to attack 1,500 Japanese defenders on Angaur.

The circumstances and the terrain between the two islands were also imbalanced. Peleliu was much larger and had a more complex landscape. The defensive fortifications were far more developed, and it offered fewer predictable landing beaches than on Angaur.

Only the later rapid shifting of plans accounted for such force allocation imbalances not being corrected at the Corps or Expeditionary Troops level. The effect of these imbalances was magnified on September 17. Higher-level changes in these plans (naval decisions) took away all the III Amphibious Corps reserves.

# DIVISIONS AND COMMANDERS

Operation Stalemate would be conducted by two divisions, one from the Marines, and one from the Army. In the Pacific since mid-1942, the 1st Marine Division was a combat-tested veteran organization that launched the first offensive landing in the Pacific on Guadalcanal.

After a brief rest and recovery in Australia, and training newly joined Marines, the division made its second amphibious assault at Cape Gloucester (Operation Backhander) on New Britain on December 26, 1943. When the 1st Division landed on Peleliu on September 15, 1944, its regiments had officers and enlisted Marine veterans from both landings and fresh troops ready to fight. Before World War II ended, the 1st Marine Division took part in one last battle: Operation Iceberg and victory on Okinawa.

## General William Rupertus

General Rupertus commanded the 1st Marine Division during their time on Peleliu. He'd been with the division since the beginning of 1942. As a brigadier general, he was General Vandegrift's assistant division commander during the Guadalcanal campaign.

He took command of the division at the start of Operation Backhander (battle for Cape Gloucester on New Britain) on December 26, 1943. Rupertus was commissioned in 1913 and commanded a Marine ship's detachment in World War I.

Following the Great War, he was assigned to duty in China and Haiti. After the Peleliu campaign, he was made Commandant of the Marine Corps schools in Quantico. On March 25, 1945, the general died of a heart attack while still on active duty, aged fifty-five.

## General Paul Mueller

General Mueller commanded the 81st Division and was a graduate of the West Point class of 1915. He commanded an infantry battalion in France in World War I and during the interwar period had several infantry commands and staff billets. In August 1941, he took command of the 81st at Fort Rucker, Alabama, and trained extensively until his division was called to battle in Angaur and Peleliu.

General Mueller served on active duty until retiring in 1954. He died ten years later on September 25 at seventy-one years of age.

## Army's 81st Infantry Division

The Wildcats formed in August 17 at Camp Jackson, South Carolina. They saw action in France at the Argonne in World War I. They were deactivated at the end of the war. In June 1942, the 81st was reactivated and sent to several Pacific training bases before their first combat assignment on Angaur.

After successful operations on Angaur, they relieved units of the 1st Marine Division on Peleliu. Once Peleliu was secure, the Wildcats trained for Operation Olympic—the invasion of Japan. But the Japanese surrendered after two atomic bomb attacks. Instead of invading Japan, the 81st became an occupying force. On January 30, 1946, the 81st Infantry Division was once again deactivated.

# JAPANESE FIGHTING TACTICS

After the December 1941 surprise attacks, Japanese military planners believed they could quickly secure an Asian empire in the Pacific. Japan would defend her territories until the bitter end. The Empire of Japan would tire and bleed out the Allies before negotiating Japanese dominance in the Pacific.

This strategic concept was in line with the medieval Japanese code of *bushido*. The Japanese believed in their army's moral superiority over lesser races. This led the Japanese to expect their 19th-century *banzai* tactics would bring them success. Experience and expectations clashed until their 1942 encounters with the Allies, particularly in the Solomon's. It took several confrontations with the Allies to learn that modern infantry weapons and tactics would defeat them.

To Allied troops, these Japanese misconceptions were disturbing but cost-effective. It was less costly and easier to mow down banzai attacks than dig stubborn defenders out of fortified positions.

By the spring of 1944, these hard lessons had been understood in the highest levels of Japan's Army Command. When General Tojo directed General Inoue to defend the Palaus deliberately and conservatively, he ordered Japanese troops to dig in and hunker down, making the final defense a costly and bloody affair.

# NAVAL GUNFIRE SUPPORT

In many of the 1st Division Marines' earlier operations (especially on Guadalcanal) they were on the receiving end of naval gunfire. At Cape Gloucester, the character and disposition of the Japanese defenses didn't call for extensive pre-landing fire support, nor did following operations ashore.

The naval gunfire Guadalcanal veterans were exposed to often damaged planes and installations onshore. Its effect on the dug-in Marines was sobering and scary, but rarely destructive.

During the planning for Peleliu, division staff had no trained naval gunfire planner. When one arrived, he was hindered by a cumbersome communications link back to higher headquarters.

General Holland M. Smith's FMF (Fleet Marine Force) in Honolulu would provide essential targeting information for the division's plan. The FMF would also plan and allocate available gunfire resources to the targets deemed necessary by the division staff planners.

This preoccupation with the ongoing Marianna's

campaigns and illness of Admiral Jesse Oldendorf, the naval gunfire support group commander, further limited and constrained preparations. Heavy enemy ammunition expenditures in the Marianas also reduced the available ammunition for the Peleliu operation.

During the delivery of Allied preparatory fires, there was no Japanese response. This persuaded Oldendorf to report all known targets destroyed and to cancel any further preparatory fires scheduled on D +3. An unintended benefit of this change in naval gunfire resulted in more shells being available for post-landing support.

But the costly effect of this inadequate naval gunfire support was that the flanking positions north and south of the landing beaches were destroyed. The selection of naval gunfire targets could have been done more thoroughly. Colonel "Chesty" Puller, the 1st Marines commander, specifically asked for the destruction of positions dominating his landing on his division's left flanks.

This failure was paid for in blood, bravery, and time during the battle for the Point.

After D-Day, there were several instances of well called and delivered naval gunfire support. Night illuminations during September 16 and the destruction of two significant blockhouses were effective support for the Ngesebus landing.

# REEF-CROSSING TACTICS

Peleliu's coral reef would not permit landing craft within 700 yards of the beach, so the landing craft deposited tanks at the reef's edge. The depth of the reef's edge allowed the tanks to operate in *most* areas without being submerged.

A plan was devised to form tanks into small columns, each led by an LVT. As long as the amphibious tractor was grounded on the reef, the tanks could follow. When an LVT encountered a depth that floated it, tanks were halted while the amphibious tractor felt for a more suitable, shallow path. This brought the tanks onshore in small columns as quickly as possible. This tactic was crucial for timely employment of armor onshore before D-Day was over.

Two other reef crossing innovations were used on D-Day. Several amphibious trailers were towed behind landing craft, and later, at the reef's edge, they were towed in by the LVTs. Once onshore, trucks pulled them the rest of the way in. This allowed for vital supplies to be brought into points in the rear of the fighting.

Newly available cranes were placed on barges near the

reef's edge. They lifted nets full of ammunition and other essential supplies from boats to tractors at the transfer lines. Crawler cranes were landed early and positioned by the shore party to lift net loads from LVTs to trucks for a swift forward delivery.

# PALAU ISLANDS

*(Berasuko Sho)*
**Velasco Reef**

*Ngaruangl Reef*

*(Kajanguru Shoto)*
**Kayangel Is**
*(Kajangle)*

*(Kosusoru Sho)*
**Kossol Reef**

*(Kosusoru Suido)*
**Kossol Passage**

*(Hokusei Sho)*
**Northwest Reef**

*(Korumoran Sho)*
**Cormoran Reef**

*(Gamegei Suido)*
**Ngamegei Passage**

*Ahnokako Pass*

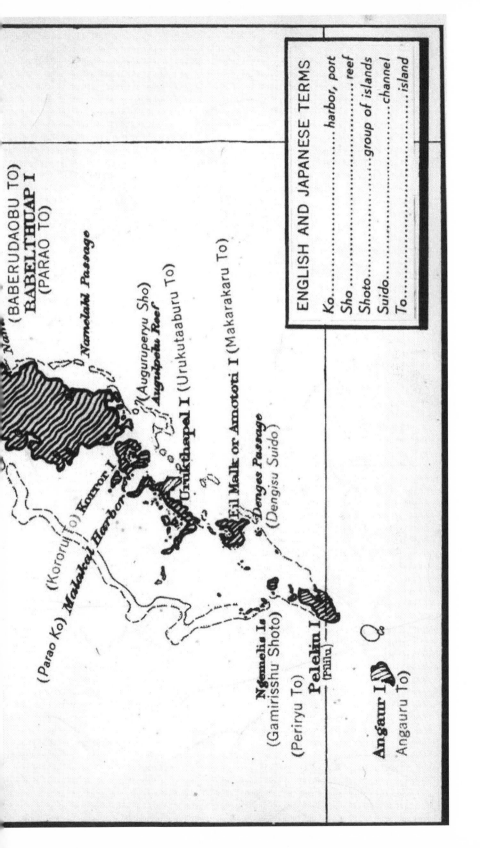

Nama (BABERUDAOBU TO)
**RABELTHUAP I**
(PARAO TO)

*Namelaki Passage*

(Auguruperyu Sho)
*Auguipelu Reef*

**Urukthapal I** (Urukutaaburu To)

**Eil Malk or Amototi I** (Makarakaru To)

*Denges Passage*
(Dengisu Suido)

(Kororu To) **Koror I**

(Parao Ko) *Malakal Harbor*

**Ngemelis Is**
(Gamirisshu Shoto)

(Peririyu To)
**Pelelin I**
(Piliu)

**Angaur I**
Angauru To)

ENGLISH AND JAPANESE TERMS

Ko........................harbor, port
Sho.................................reef
Shoto................group of islands
Suido..........................channel
To.................................island

# CONQUEST OF PELELIU

Was the seizure of Peleliu necessary?

What were the advantages to the US war effort from securing Peleliu?

It assured the absolute domination of all the Palau Islands. It also added to the security of General MacArthur's right flank as he continued westward with his Philippines campaign. Within the Palaus group, the conquest destroyed enemy facilities that survived Admiral Mitscher's destructive strike in March 1944.

Securing Peleliu also ensured a total denial of support to Japanese forces from the submarine base at Koror. Reducing the already waning enemy submarine capability east of the Philippines.

The Allied position on Peleliu contributed to neutralizing 25,000 enemy troops in northern Palau. The Peleliu landing *did not* contribute to the RLT 323's (regimental landing team) unopposed seizure of Ulithi. Admiral Halsey had earlier believed his forces could seize Ulithi without first taking Peleliu.

The most significant visible benefit of a subdued Peleliu was its use as a link in the flight path and communication lines from Hawaii to the Philippines. It was convenient but not a necessity.

Survivors of the *Indianapolis* during the July 29, 1945 sinking were saved indirectly by the seizure of Peleliu. After delivering atomic bomb parts to Tinian, the ship was heading for the Philippines when it was torpedoed. The *Indianapolis* sunk in twelve minutes. There was no received report of the contact or the sinking. Four days after it sunk, the 316 survivors (from a crew of 1,197) were spotted by a Navy patrol bomber flying out of Peleliu. This sighting directly led to the rescue and most likely would not have happened but for the Allied occupation of Peleliu.

# PRICE OF PELELIU

Marine Casualties were 6,526. This included Navy doctors and corpsmen with 1,252 killed. The Army's 81st Division had 3,088 casualties, 404 were killed in action. Total US troop casualties were 9,616 (1,657 killed) on Peleliu, Angaur, and Ngesebus

The Japanese were successful in implementing their bleed and delay strategy. Their actions cost them an estimated 11,000 casualties (all but a small portion killed). Only 202 prisoners of war were captured, and of them, only nineteen were Japanese military (twelve Navy and seven Army). The rest were Korean laborers. Statistically, less than two out of every thousand Japanese military defenders were captured.

The bloody battle at Peleliu was a warning for the remaining Allied operations being conducted across the Pacific. Even with total naval and air superiority and a four to one troop advantage—the conquest of Peleliu cost one Allied casualty and 1,590 rounds of ammunition per Japanese soldier killed or driven from his position. A couple of months later, the attacks on Iwo Jima and Okinawa would confirm this grim calculation.

On September 13, 1944, two days before D-Day, Admiral Halsey recommended to Admiral Nimitz that the Peleliu landing should be canceled. But by that time, it was too late: Peleliu would be added to the long list of brutal battles in which Allied forces fought, suffered, and ultimately prevailed.

Seventy-seven years later, the question of whether Operation Stalemate was necessary remains debatable. The heroism and commendable conduct of the 1st Marine Division, its Navy corpsmen, and soldiers of the 81st Infantry on that miserable island will forever be written in blood.

\* \* \*

Building a relationship with my readers is one of the best things about writing. I occasionally send out emails with details on new releases and special offers. If you'd like to join my free readers group and never miss a new release, go to danielwrinn.com to sign up for the list.

# REFERENCES

Anderson, Charles R. *Western Pacific*. The U.S. Army Campaigns of World War II. U.S. Army Center of Military History, 1994. CMH Pub 72-29.

Burbeck, James. "Invasion of Peleliu". *Animated Combat Map*. The War Times Journal, 2008

Chen, C. Peter "Palau Islands and Ulithi Islands Campaign". *World War II Database*. Archived from the original on October 6, 2007.

Gayle, Gordon D., BGen USMC. *Bloody Beaches: the Marines at Peleliu*. Washington, D.C.: Marine Corp Historical Center, 1996.

Gypton, Jeremy. "Bloody Peleliu". MilitaryHistoryOnline, 2008.

Hallas, James H. *The Devil's Anvil: The Assault on Peleliu*. Praeger Publishers, 1994

Hastings, Max. *Retribution: the Battle for Japan, 1944-45*. New York: Alfred A. Knopf, 2009.

Hough, Frank O. *The Assault on Peleliu*. Washington, D.C.: Historical Division, Headquarters, U.S. Marine Corps, 1950.

Moran, Jim, and Gordon L. Rottman. *Peleliu 1944: the Forgotten Corner of Hell*. Oxford: Osprey, 2002.

Morison, Samuel Eliot. *Leyte: June 1944-January 1945, vol. 12*. Boston: Little, Brown and Company, 1958.

Ross, Bill D. *Peleliu: Tragic Triumph: the Untold Story of the Pacific War's Forgotten Battle*. New York: Random House, 1991.

Shread, Paul. "The Battle of Peleliu and the scars of war". *The Concord Monitor*. Archived from the original on September 19, 2014.

Sledge, E. B. *With the Old Breed: At Peleliu and Okinawa*. New York: Oxford University Press, 1991.

Sloan, Bill. *Brotherhood of Heroes: the Marines at Peleliu, 1944: the Bloodiest Battle of the Pacific War*. New York: Simon & Schuster, 2005.

Wright, Derrick. *To the Far Side of Hell: the Battle for Peleliu, 1944*. Tuscaloosa: University of Alabama Press, 2005.

# ALSO BY DANIEL WRINN

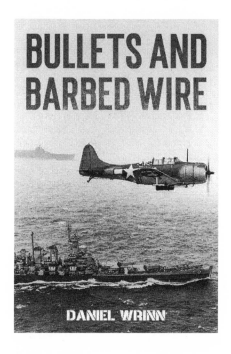

BULLETS AND BARBED WIRE : FROM GUADALCANAL TO CAPE
GLOUCESTER

*"A thoughtful and gripping account of the beginnings of the War in the Pacific."* – Reviewer

## Discover a newfound appreciation for the war in the Pacific.

From the shores of Cape Gloucester to the quiet atolls and islands of the Solomon Sea, the Second World War left a profound mark on this sheltered corner of the globe, which would be felt for decades to come. Caught in the center of a vicious struggle between two superpowers, these islands would form an unconventional battleground for the US Marines and the Japanese Navy.

This book offers you a new look at the WWII Pacific Theater, providing an enlightening glimpse into the battles and campaigns during the Allied offensive. With a breakdown of three significant US campaigns:

• **Operation Watchtower,** a riveting exploration of the spark that set off the Allied offensive in the Pacific islands, detailing the gruelling struggle for the island of Guadalcanal and its vital strategic position

• **Operation Galvanic,** an incredible account of the battle for the Tarawa Atoll and base that would give them a stepping stone into the heart of Japanese-controlled waters

• And **Operation Backhander,** which offers a gripping retelling of the war for Cape Gloucester, New Guinea, and the Bismarck Sea

Each of these momentous operations are fascinating feats of strategy, planning, and bravery, handing the Allies what would eventually become a victory over the Pacific Theater and an end to Imperialist Japanese expansion. This brilliant book sheds light on this often-overlooked facet of WWII, providing students, history fans, and World War II buffs alike with a captivating breakdown of history and combat that defined the beginning of the US offensive in the Pacific.

OPERATION FORAGER: 1944 BATTLE FOR SAIPAN, INVASION OF
TINIAN, AND RECAPTURE OF GUAM

*"History buffs and newbie history buffs alike will love this book."*
—Reviewer

## A gripping account of one of the most daring—and disturbing—operations in the Pacific war.

From the heavy fighting in Saipan to the securing of Tinian and Guam, the Pacific war left its profound mark in this sheltered corner of the world, which would be felt for several decades to come. Caught in the center of a vicious struggle between two superpowers, these islands would form an unconventional battleground for US forces and the Japanese Navy.

This book offers you a new look at the WWII Pacific Theater, providing an enlightening glimpse into the battles and campaigns during the Allied offensive. With a breakdown of three significant US campaigns:

- **Battle for Saipan**, since the fall of the Marshall Islands a few months earlier, both sides prepared for an American onslaught against the Marianas and Saipan in particular.
- **Invasion of Tinian**, is the incredible account of the assault on Tinian. Located just under six miles southwest of Saipan. This was the first use of napalm and the "shore to shore" concept.
- **Recapture of Guam**, offers a gripping retelling of the recapture of the Japanese-held island of Guam, captured by the Japanese in 1941 during one of the first Pacific campaigns of the War.

Each of these momentous operations are fascinating feats of strategy, planning, and bravery, handing the Allies what would eventually become a victory over the Pacific Theater and an end to Imperialist Japanese expansion.

This brilliant book sheds light on this often-overlooked facet of WWII, providing students, history fans, and World War II buffs alike with a captivating breakdown of history and combat that defined the US offensive in the Pacific.

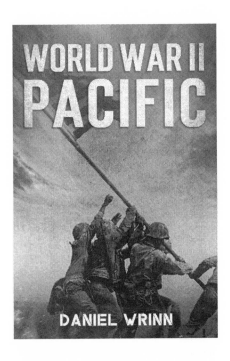

WORLD WAR II PACIFIC: BATTLES AND CAMPAIGNS FROM
GUADALCANAL TO OKINAWA 1942-1945

*"A brisk and compelling game changer for the historiography of the Pacific
Theater in World War II."* – Reviewer

**An enlightening glimpse into nine battles and
campaigns during the Pacific War Allied offensive.**

Each of these momentous operations were fascinating feats
of strategy, planning, and bravery, handing the Allies what
would eventually become a victory over the Pacific Theater
and an end to Imperialist Japanese expansion.

**Operation Watchtower,** a riveting exploration of the
spark that set off the Allied offensive in the Pacific islands,
detailing the grueling struggle for the island of Guadalcanal
and its vital strategic position.

**Operation Galvanic,** an incredible account of the battle

for the Tarawa Atoll and base that would give them a stepping-stone into the heart of Japanese-controlled waters.

**Operation Backhander**, a gripping retelling of the war for Cape Gloucester, New Guinea, and the Bismarck Sea.

**Battle for Saipan**, Marines stormed the beaches with a goal of gaining a crucial air base from which the US could launch its new long-range B-29 bombers directly at Japan's home islands.

**Invasion of Tinian**, is the incredible account of the assault on Tinian. Located just under six miles southwest of Saipan. This was the first use of napalm and the "shore to shore" concept.

**Recapture of Guam**, a gripping narrative about the liberation of the Japanese-held island of Guam, captured by the Japanese in 1941 during one of the first Pacific campaigns of the War.

**Operation Stalemate**, Marines landed on the island of Peleliu, one of the Palau Islands in the Pacific, as part of a larger operation to provide support for General MacArthur, who was preparing to invade the Philippines.

**Operation Detachment**, the battle of Iwo Jima was a major offensive in World War II. The Marine invasion was tasked with the mission of capturing airfields on the island for use by P-51 fighters.

**Operation Iceberg**, the invasion and ultimate victory on Okinawa was the largest amphibious assault in the Pacific Theater. It was also one of the bloodiest battles in the Pacific, lasting ninety-eight days.

This gripping narrative sheds light on these often-overlooked facets of WWII, providing students, history fans, and World War II buffs alike with a captivating breakdown of the history and combat that defined the ultimate victory of US forces in the Pacific.

# ABOUT THE AUTHOR

Daniel Wrinn writes Military History & War Stories. A US Navy veteran and avid history buff, Daniel lives in the Utah Wasatch Mountains. He writes every day with a view of the snow capped peaks of Park City to keep him company. You can join his readers group and get notified of new releases, special offers, and free books here:

www.danielwrinn.com

Made in the USA
Monee, IL
01 July 2021